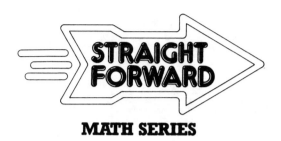

MATH SERIES

ADVANCED
FRACTIONS

by S. Harold Collins

Book design by Kathy Kifer.

Copyright © 1988 Stanley H. Collins

Published by:
Garlic Press
605 Powers St.
Eugene, OR 97402

ISBN 0-931993-21-0
Order Number GP-021

www.garlicpress.com

To Parents and Teachers,

The Advanced Straight Forward Math Series has been designed for parents and teachers of children. This is the advanced fractions book. It is a straightforward, sequenced presentation of advanced fraction skills. It assumes that basis math facts have already been mastered. If not, consult our first series: **The Straight Forward Math Series.**

These steps are suggested for mastery of advanced fraction skills:

- Give the **Beginning Assessment Test** to determine where to begin the Practice Sheets. The Beginning Assessment Test (page 1) will tell which basic fraction skills are sound and which need attention. Begin the Practice Sheets where the Beginning Assessment Test indicates that fraction errors start.

  Look at the Beginning Assessment Test. If you consult the Answers beginning on page 28, you will see that the problems to this test are arranged in groupings. Each grouping is a skill. Each skill is sequential and requires mastery before a higher skill level can be started.

- Start the **Practice Sheets** at the appropriate skill level as detemined from the Beginning Assessment Test. Do not skip levels once begun; build to mastery for all new skills.

  Practice Sheets are given for each skill level to provide ample practice.

  Set a standard to move from one skill level to the next; either a percentage correct or a number correct.

- Give a **Section Diagnostic Test** as a final measure of a particular section. Section Diagnostic Tests are arranged to identify any problems which may still exist with a particular skill (much like the Beginning Assessment Test).

  Set a standard to move from one section to the next. If that standard is not met, go back, focus on problem skills with Practice Sheets or similar materials.

- Give the **Final Assessment Test** to measure all advanced fraction skills. Compare the change from the Beginning Assessment Test.

Contents

A Breath of Fresh Air
GarlicPress

Beginning Assessment Test

Write an Equivalent Fraction	Reduce	Change to Mixed Numbers	Write as Improper Fraction
$\frac{1}{2} =$	$\frac{5}{10} =$	$\frac{5}{4} =$	$2\frac{1}{2} =$
$\frac{1}{5} =$	$\frac{4}{6} =$	$\frac{10}{7} =$	$6\frac{1}{8} =$
$\frac{3}{4} =$	$\frac{16}{20} =$	$\frac{20}{12} =$	$4\frac{3}{15} =$
$\frac{1}{3} =$	$\frac{3}{12} =$	$\frac{14}{4} =$	$5\frac{7}{8} =$

Addition. Reduce when necessary.

$$\begin{array}{r} \frac{3}{4} \\ + \frac{3}{4} \\ \hline \end{array}$$

$$\frac{1}{8} + \frac{4}{8} =$$

$$\frac{1}{8} + \frac{1}{2} =$$

$$\begin{array}{r} 8\frac{1}{2} \\ + 4\frac{1}{6} \\ \hline \end{array}$$

$$\frac{1}{3} + \frac{1}{6} =$$

$$2\frac{3}{8} + 2\frac{3}{8} =$$

$$\begin{array}{r} 24\frac{1}{2} \\ +17\frac{2}{3} \\ \hline \end{array}$$

Subtraction. Reduce when necessary.

$$\frac{2}{3} - \frac{2}{3} =$$

$$\frac{8}{9} - \frac{4}{9} =$$

$$\begin{array}{r} \frac{1}{2} \\ - \frac{1}{4} \\ \hline \end{array}$$

$$\begin{array}{r} \frac{3}{8} \\ - \frac{1}{4} \\ \hline \end{array}$$

$$\begin{array}{r} 15 \\ - 4\frac{2}{5} \\ \hline \end{array}$$

$$\begin{array}{r} 10\frac{3}{8} \\ - 4\frac{3}{4} \\ \hline \end{array}$$

Multiplication. Reduce when necessary.

$$\frac{1}{2} \times \frac{1}{3} =$$

$$\frac{3}{5} \times 5 =$$

$$5\frac{1}{4} \times \frac{2}{9} =$$

$$4\frac{1}{6} \times 2\frac{2}{5} =$$

Division. Reduce when necessary.

$$\frac{1}{4} \div \frac{1}{2} =$$

$$\frac{3}{8} \div \frac{3}{4} =$$

$$1\frac{5}{8} \div 1\frac{1}{4} =$$

$$2\frac{1}{2} \div \frac{1}{2} =$$

1

Equivalent Fractions.

$\frac{1}{2} = \frac{}{4}$

$\frac{1}{8} = \frac{}{24}$

$\frac{2}{9} = \frac{}{18} = \frac{}{27}$

$\frac{1}{4} = \frac{}{12} = \frac{}{16} = \frac{}{20}$

$\frac{1}{4} = \frac{}{8}$

$\frac{3}{4} = \frac{}{8}$

$\frac{2}{3} = \frac{}{6} = \frac{}{9}$

$\frac{3}{4} = \frac{}{12} = \frac{}{16} = \frac{}{24}$

$\frac{1}{3} = \frac{}{9}$

$\frac{2}{7} = \frac{}{14}$

$\frac{2}{5} = \frac{}{10} = \frac{}{15}$

$\frac{1}{2} = \frac{}{50} = \frac{}{100} = \frac{}{200}$

$\frac{1}{5} = \frac{}{10}$

$\frac{11}{12} = \frac{}{24}$

$\frac{5}{6} = \frac{}{12} = \frac{}{18}$

$\frac{7}{8} = \frac{}{16} = \frac{}{24} = \frac{}{32}$

$\frac{1}{6} = \frac{}{12}$

$\frac{3}{5} = \frac{}{15}$

$\frac{25}{100} = \frac{}{200} = \frac{}{300}$

$\frac{7}{10} = \frac{}{40} = \frac{}{50} = \frac{}{80}$

$\frac{1}{10} = \frac{}{30}$

$\frac{22}{25} = \frac{}{50}$

$\frac{2}{50} = \frac{}{100} = \frac{}{150}$

$\frac{50}{100} = \frac{}{300} = \frac{}{400} = \frac{}{1000}$

Reduce to Lowest Terms.

$\frac{16}{20} = \frac{}{10} = \frac{}{5}$

$\frac{50}{100} =$

$\frac{5}{20} =$

$\frac{11}{33} =$

$\frac{4}{12} = \frac{}{6} = \frac{}{3}$

$\frac{12}{30} =$

$\frac{3}{9} =$

$\frac{20}{30} =$

$\frac{12}{16} = \frac{}{8} = \frac{}{4}$

$\frac{16}{18} =$

$\frac{8}{18} =$

$\frac{7}{28} =$

$\frac{5}{10} =$

$\frac{14}{21} =$

$\frac{24}{36} =$

$\frac{30}{48} =$

$\frac{6}{9} =$

$\frac{6}{10} =$

$\frac{150}{250} =$

$\frac{25}{75} =$

$\frac{9}{10} =$

$\frac{16}{34} =$

$\frac{14}{16} =$

$\frac{10}{14} =$

$\frac{3}{12} =$

$\frac{6}{14} =$

$\frac{15}{60} =$

$\frac{10}{42} =$

proper & improper fractions

Change to Mixed Numbers. Reduce.

$\frac{4}{3}=$	$\frac{14}{3}=$	$\frac{48}{5}=$	$\frac{17}{4}=$
$\frac{16}{8}=$	$\frac{14}{4}=$	$\frac{15}{2}=$	$\frac{28}{8}=$
$\frac{8}{5}=$	$\frac{20}{12}=$	$\frac{68}{11}=$	$\frac{39}{10}=$
$\frac{11}{2}=$	$\frac{10}{6}=$	$\frac{29}{12}=$	$\frac{27}{5}=$
$\frac{10}{7}=$	$\frac{22}{7}=$	$\frac{55}{27}=$	$\frac{84}{9}=$
$\frac{9}{4}=$	$\frac{20}{15}=$	$\frac{43}{9}=$	$\frac{47}{6}=$
$\frac{6}{6}=$	$\frac{45}{20}=$	$\frac{100}{33}=$	$\frac{30}{12}=$
$\frac{15}{12}=$	$\frac{13}{8}=$	$\frac{60}{20}=$	$\frac{60}{5}=$

Change to Improper Fractions.

$2\frac{1}{2}=$	$3\frac{3}{16}=$	$7\frac{3}{8}=$	$4\frac{3}{4}=$
$4\frac{1}{3}=$	$5\frac{8}{9}=$	$8\frac{2}{3}=$	$7\frac{2}{11}=$
$5\frac{3}{4}=$	$4\frac{5}{12}=$	$5\frac{1}{12}=$	$3\frac{3}{16}=$
$3\frac{9}{10}=$	$9\frac{1}{4}=$	$3\frac{6}{7}=$	$5\frac{2}{3}=$
$6\frac{1}{8}=$	$3\frac{2}{15}=$	$4\frac{3}{15}=$	$5\frac{7}{8}=$
$7\frac{2}{5}=$	$6\frac{5}{6}=$	$6\frac{4}{5}=$	$9\frac{6}{7}=$
$1\frac{2}{3}=$	$2\frac{11}{12}=$	$4\frac{4}{9}=$	$2\frac{11}{12}=$
$2\frac{3}{7}=$	$8\frac{1}{2}=$	$6\frac{7}{10}=$	$7\frac{1}{9}=$

Fraction Addition

Reduce to Lowest Terms when necessary.

$\frac{1}{4} + \frac{1}{4} =$ $\frac{1}{8} + \frac{4}{8} =$ $\frac{5}{10} + \frac{3}{10} =$ $\frac{4}{12} + \frac{7}{12} =$ $\frac{2}{5} + \frac{2}{5} =$

$\frac{7}{16} + \frac{9}{16} =$ $\frac{1}{4} + \frac{2}{4} =$ $\frac{5}{11} + \frac{3}{11} =$ $\frac{4}{6} + \frac{3}{6} =$ $\frac{8}{10} + \frac{7}{10} =$

$\frac{7}{9} + \frac{1}{9} =$ $\frac{5}{15} + \frac{5}{15} =$ $\frac{5}{8} + \frac{4}{8} =$ $\frac{3}{7} + \frac{3}{7} =$ $\frac{3}{12} + \frac{6}{12} =$

$\frac{10}{16} + \frac{4}{16} =$ $\frac{2}{10} + \frac{9}{10} =$ $\frac{1}{4} + \frac{3}{4} =$ $\frac{7}{8} + \frac{7}{8} =$ $\frac{4}{9} + \frac{2}{9} =$

$1\frac{3}{4} + 1\frac{3}{4} =$ $\frac{15}{16} + \frac{15}{16} =$ $\frac{10}{11} + 1\frac{5}{11} =$ $2\frac{3}{8} + 3\frac{3}{8} =$ $\frac{5}{6} + 1 =$

$\begin{array}{r} \frac{3}{4} \\ + \frac{3}{4} \\ \hline \end{array}$ $\begin{array}{r} \frac{7}{8} \\ + \frac{5}{8} \\ \hline \end{array}$ $\begin{array}{r} \frac{1}{2} \\ + 1\frac{1}{2} \\ \hline \end{array}$ $\begin{array}{r} \frac{5}{11} \\ + \frac{7}{11} \\ \hline \end{array}$ $\begin{array}{r} \frac{7}{10} \\ + \frac{5}{10} \\ \hline \end{array}$ $\begin{array}{r} \frac{5}{16} \\ + \frac{7}{16} \\ \hline \end{array}$

$\begin{array}{r} 1\frac{4}{15} \\ + 2\frac{3}{15} \\ \hline \end{array}$ $\begin{array}{r} \frac{7}{12} \\ + \frac{5}{12} \\ \hline \end{array}$ $\begin{array}{r} 3\frac{5}{6} \\ + 2\frac{5}{6} \\ \hline \end{array}$ $\begin{array}{r} 1\frac{9}{20} \\ + \frac{9}{20} \\ \hline \end{array}$ $\begin{array}{r} \frac{7}{18} \\ + \frac{13}{18} \\ \hline \end{array}$ $\begin{array}{r} \frac{10}{25} \\ + 4\frac{10}{25} \\ \hline \end{array}$

$\begin{array}{r} 6\frac{11}{16} \\ + 3\frac{4}{16} \\ \hline \end{array}$ $\begin{array}{r} 2\frac{8}{15} \\ + 2\frac{6}{15} \\ \hline \end{array}$ $\begin{array}{r} \frac{11}{20} \\ + \frac{8}{20} \\ \hline \end{array}$ $\begin{array}{r} 5\frac{6}{7} \\ + 4\frac{4}{7} \\ \hline \end{array}$ $\begin{array}{r} 1\frac{7}{24} \\ + \frac{11}{24} \\ \hline \end{array}$ $\begin{array}{r} \frac{15}{16} \\ + 7\frac{2}{16} \\ \hline \end{array}$

Fraction Addition

unlike denominators

Reduce to Lowest Terms when necessary.

$\frac{1}{4}$
$+\ \frac{1}{2}$

$\frac{1}{3}$
$+\ \frac{1}{6}$

$\frac{3}{8}$
$+\ \frac{1}{4}$

$\frac{2}{5}$
$+\ \frac{3}{10}$

$\frac{1}{8}$
$+\ \frac{1}{2}$

$\frac{2}{9}$
$+\ \frac{2}{3}$

$\frac{1}{2}$
$+\ \frac{1}{6}$

$\frac{3}{4}$
$+\ \frac{1}{8}$

$\frac{2}{3}$
$+\ \frac{1}{4}$

$\frac{1}{2}$
$+\ \frac{2}{5}$

$\frac{3}{10}$
$+\ \frac{4}{5}$

$\frac{3}{4}$
$+\ \frac{3}{8}$

$\frac{2}{7}$
$+\ \frac{1}{2}$

$\frac{1}{6}$
$+\ \frac{3}{4}$

$\frac{10}{15}$
$+\ \frac{2}{5}$

$\frac{1}{2}$
$+\ \frac{4}{9}$

$\frac{2}{3}$
$+\ \frac{3}{5}$

$\frac{3}{4}$
$+\ \frac{3}{12}$

$\frac{5}{6}$
$+\ \frac{1}{18}$

$\frac{1}{3}$
$+\ \frac{5}{6}$

$\frac{3}{4}$
$+\ \frac{5}{6}$

$\frac{1}{3}$
$+\ \frac{2}{7}$

$\frac{5}{12}$
$+\ \frac{3}{8}$

$\frac{3}{5}$
$+\ \frac{1}{6}$

Fraction Addition

unlike denominators

Reduce to Lowest Terms when necessary.

$$\frac{5}{8} + \frac{5}{6}$$
$$\frac{7}{12} + \frac{2}{9}$$
$$\frac{1}{4} + \frac{3}{10}$$
$$\frac{5}{6} + \frac{1}{2}$$

$$\frac{3}{4} + \frac{5}{9}$$
$$\frac{1}{3} + \frac{5}{6}$$
$$\frac{1}{2} + \frac{3}{7}$$
$$\frac{5}{6} + \frac{4}{7}$$

$$\frac{2}{3} + \frac{1}{7}$$
$$\frac{3}{10} + \frac{1}{5}$$
$$\frac{1}{8} + \frac{4}{9}$$
$$\frac{3}{5} + \frac{3}{4}$$

$$\frac{1}{2} + \frac{1}{4} + \frac{3}{8}$$
$$\frac{7}{12} + \frac{3}{4} + \frac{1}{3}$$
$$\frac{1}{2} + \frac{1}{3} + \frac{5}{6}$$
$$\frac{2}{9} + \frac{1}{2} + \frac{2}{3}$$

$$\frac{2}{3} + \frac{3}{5} + \frac{13}{15}$$
$$\frac{3}{8} + \frac{1}{6} + \frac{3}{12}$$
$$\frac{3}{10} + \frac{1}{6} + \frac{2}{5}$$
$$\frac{1}{2} + \frac{3}{7} + \frac{3}{4}$$

Fraction Addition

fractions, mixed numbers, and whole numbers

Reduce to Lowest Terms when necessary.

$8\frac{1}{2}$
$+\ 4\frac{1}{6}$

$5\frac{7}{10}$
$+12\frac{1}{2}$

$2\frac{1}{9}$
$+10\frac{2}{3}$

$6\frac{4}{7}$
$+\ 5\frac{12}{14}$

$12\frac{3}{4}$
$+\ 6\frac{1}{7}$

$75\frac{2}{3}$
$+12\frac{3}{4}$

$21\frac{1}{2}$
$+19\frac{2}{5}$

$15\frac{7}{12}$
$+\ 5\frac{3}{18}$

$9\frac{4}{10}$
$+\ 6\frac{3}{20}$

$12\frac{1}{3}$
$+\ 7\frac{7}{15}$

$24\frac{1}{8}$
$+18\frac{3}{4}$

$6\frac{4}{9}$
$+11\frac{3}{18}$

$10\frac{1}{2}$
$+41\frac{5}{12}$

$18\frac{1}{3}$
$+12\frac{5}{7}$

$60\frac{4}{7}$
$+\ 12\frac{10}{14}$

$11\frac{1}{3}$
$+\ 9\frac{1}{2}$

$5\frac{1}{4}$
$+21\frac{2}{5}$

$32\frac{1}{6}$
$+\ 3\frac{3}{4}$

$17\frac{3}{8}$
$+14\frac{1}{3}$

$15\frac{1}{2}$
$+\ 6\frac{11}{12}$

$12\frac{7}{12}$
$+\ 2\frac{3}{4}$

$29\frac{3}{5}$
$+11\frac{1}{8}$

$47\frac{4}{5}$
$+12\frac{2}{3}$

$17\frac{3}{4}$
$+\ 5\frac{1}{6}$

7

Fraction Addition

mixed & whole numbers

Reduce to Lowest Terms when necessary.

$$74\tfrac{1}{2}$$
$$+16\tfrac{3}{8}$$

$$12\tfrac{5}{6}$$
$$+32\tfrac{3}{8}$$

$$24\tfrac{1}{2}$$
$$+17\tfrac{2}{3}$$

$$17\tfrac{3}{4}$$
$$+20\tfrac{3}{5}$$

$$42\tfrac{5}{12}$$
$$+\ 6\tfrac{7}{8}$$

$$14\tfrac{1}{2}$$
$$+27\tfrac{4}{9}$$

$$29\tfrac{3}{16}$$
$$+14\tfrac{1}{4}$$

$$81\tfrac{2}{7}$$
$$+\ 3\tfrac{5}{6}$$

$$38\tfrac{9}{10}$$
$$+14\tfrac{1}{2}$$

$$18\tfrac{1}{3}$$
$$+17\tfrac{5}{7}$$

$$44\tfrac{3}{5}$$
$$+42\tfrac{1}{6}$$

$$57\tfrac{7}{11}$$
$$+12\tfrac{1}{3}$$

$$60\tfrac{1}{8}$$
$$+47\tfrac{2}{5}$$

$$15\tfrac{1}{15}$$
$$+27\tfrac{1}{2}$$

$$17\tfrac{3}{4}$$
$$+18\tfrac{5}{12}$$

$$37\tfrac{2}{7}$$
$$+10\tfrac{3}{4}$$

$$52\tfrac{3}{18}$$
$$+12\tfrac{4}{9}$$

$$68\tfrac{5}{8}$$
$$+\ 9\tfrac{1}{3}$$

$$18\tfrac{2}{3}$$
$$+39\tfrac{5}{8}$$

$$24\tfrac{1}{2}$$
$$+17\tfrac{7}{8}$$

$$34\tfrac{7}{10}$$
$$+16\tfrac{3}{4}$$

$$11\tfrac{1}{2}$$
$$+41\tfrac{3}{5}$$

$$74\tfrac{1}{16}$$
$$+38\tfrac{3}{8}$$

$$6\tfrac{3}{8}$$
$$+\ 7\tfrac{12}{32}$$

Section Diagnostic Test

addition

Reduce to Lowest Terms when necessary.

$\frac{1}{7} + \frac{3}{7} =$ $\frac{5}{10} + \frac{3}{10} =$ $\frac{3}{8} + \frac{5}{8} =$ $\frac{5}{6} + \frac{5}{6} =$

$\frac{5}{12} + \frac{1}{12} =$ $\frac{4}{9} + \frac{2}{9} =$ $\frac{7}{16} + \frac{11}{16} =$ $\frac{1}{11} + \frac{8}{11} =$

$\begin{array}{r} \frac{1}{2} \\ + \frac{3}{4} \\ \hline \end{array}$ $\begin{array}{r} \frac{1}{3} \\ + \frac{1}{6} \\ \hline \end{array}$ $\begin{array}{r} \frac{5}{12} \\ + \frac{3}{4} \\ \hline \end{array}$ $\begin{array}{r} \frac{3}{8} \\ + \frac{1}{4} \\ \hline \end{array}$

$\begin{array}{r} \frac{1}{6} \\ + \frac{3}{4} \\ \hline \end{array}$ $\begin{array}{r} \frac{1}{4} \\ + \frac{3}{5} \\ \hline \end{array}$ $\begin{array}{r} \frac{7}{10} \\ + \frac{3}{4} \\ \hline \end{array}$ $\begin{array}{r} \frac{1}{4} \\ + \frac{5}{6} \\ \hline \end{array}$

$\begin{array}{r} 45\frac{1}{2} \\ +17\frac{2}{5} \\ \hline \end{array}$ $\begin{array}{r} 23\frac{1}{8} \\ +12\frac{1}{3} \\ \hline \end{array}$ $\begin{array}{r} 50\frac{9}{10} \\ + 2\frac{5}{6} \\ \hline \end{array}$ $\begin{array}{r} 12\frac{3}{7} \\ +15\frac{1}{6} \\ \hline \end{array}$

$\begin{array}{r} 14\frac{13}{18} \\ +17\frac{4}{9} \\ \hline \end{array}$ $\begin{array}{r} 20\frac{1}{2} \\ +12\frac{3}{7} \\ \hline \end{array}$ $\begin{array}{r} 86\frac{2}{3} \\ +12\frac{4}{7} \\ \hline \end{array}$ $\begin{array}{r} 91\frac{3}{8} \\ + 6\frac{2}{3} \\ \hline \end{array}$

like denominators

Reduce to Lowest Terms when necessary.

$\dfrac{7}{9} - \dfrac{4}{9} =$ $\qquad$ $\dfrac{4}{5} - \dfrac{2}{5} =$ $\qquad$ $\dfrac{6}{7} - \dfrac{3}{7} =$ $\qquad$ $\dfrac{3}{4} - \dfrac{1}{4} =$ $\qquad$ $\dfrac{7}{10} - \dfrac{6}{10} =$

$\dfrac{9}{11} - \dfrac{6}{11} =$ $\qquad$ $\dfrac{8}{9} - \dfrac{4}{9} =$ $\qquad$ $\dfrac{11}{12} - \dfrac{3}{12} =$ $\qquad$ $\dfrac{13}{16} - \dfrac{5}{16} =$ $\qquad$ $\dfrac{5}{14} - \dfrac{3}{14} =$

$\dfrac{2}{3} - \dfrac{2}{3} =$ $\qquad$ $\dfrac{12}{19} - \dfrac{11}{19} =$ $\qquad$ $\dfrac{11}{15} - \dfrac{6}{15} =$ $\qquad$ $\dfrac{10}{21} - \dfrac{1}{21} =$ $\qquad$ $\dfrac{7}{9} - \dfrac{4}{9} =$

$\dfrac{3}{20} - \dfrac{1}{20} =$ $\qquad$ $\dfrac{7}{8} - \dfrac{5}{8} =$ $\qquad$ $\dfrac{15}{24} - \dfrac{9}{24} =$ $\qquad$ $\dfrac{11}{12} - \dfrac{9}{12} =$ $\qquad$ $\dfrac{11}{18} - \dfrac{7}{18} =$

$\dfrac{17}{25} - \dfrac{12}{25} =$ $\qquad$ $\dfrac{8}{15} - \dfrac{7}{15} =$ $\qquad$ $\dfrac{9}{16} - \dfrac{3}{16} =$ $\qquad$ $\dfrac{14}{15} - \dfrac{7}{15} =$ $\qquad$ $\dfrac{9}{10} - \dfrac{3}{10} =$

$\begin{array}{r} \frac{3}{4} \\ -\ \frac{1}{4} \\ \hline \end{array}$ $\qquad$ $\begin{array}{r} \frac{5}{8} \\ -\ \frac{3}{8} \\ \hline \end{array}$ $\qquad$ $\begin{array}{r} \frac{11}{12} \\ -\ \frac{1}{12} \\ \hline \end{array}$ $\qquad$ $\begin{array}{r} \frac{9}{11} \\ -\ \frac{3}{11} \\ \hline \end{array}$ $\qquad$ $\begin{array}{r} \frac{17}{20} \\ -\ \frac{7}{20} \\ \hline \end{array}$

$\begin{array}{r} \frac{15}{16} \\ -\ \frac{9}{16} \\ \hline \end{array}$ $\qquad$ $\begin{array}{r} \frac{10}{21} \\ -\ \frac{3}{21} \\ \hline \end{array}$ $\qquad$ $\begin{array}{r} \frac{11}{15} \\ -\ \frac{4}{15} \\ \hline \end{array}$ $\qquad$ $\begin{array}{r} \frac{15}{16} \\ -\ \frac{7}{16} \\ \hline \end{array}$ $\qquad$ $\begin{array}{r} \frac{8}{9} \\ -\ \frac{5}{9} \\ \hline \end{array}$

$\begin{array}{r} \frac{9}{10} \\ -\ \frac{7}{10} \\ \hline \end{array}$ $\qquad$ $\begin{array}{r} \frac{15}{16} \\ -\ \frac{8}{16} \\ \hline \end{array}$ $\qquad$ $\begin{array}{r} \frac{27}{30} \\ -\ \frac{15}{30} \\ \hline \end{array}$ $\qquad$ $\begin{array}{r} \frac{8}{15} \\ -\ \frac{6}{15} \\ \hline \end{array}$ $\qquad$ $\begin{array}{r} \frac{15}{18} \\ -\ \frac{13}{18} \\ \hline \end{array}$

unlike denominators

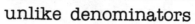

Reduce to Lowest Terms when necessary.

$$\frac{1}{2} - \frac{1}{4}$$

$$\frac{1}{3} - \frac{1}{6}$$

$$\frac{3}{8} - \frac{1}{4}$$

$$\frac{2}{5} - \frac{3}{10}$$

$$\frac{5}{8} - \frac{1}{2}$$

$$\frac{2}{3} - \frac{2}{9}$$

$$\frac{1}{2} - \frac{3}{6}$$

$$\frac{4}{5} - \frac{8}{15}$$

$$\frac{2}{3} - \frac{1}{4}$$

$$\frac{6}{7} - \frac{1}{3}$$

$$\frac{5}{6} - \frac{3}{4}$$

$$\frac{7}{8} - \frac{3}{4}$$

$$\frac{11}{12} - \frac{3}{8}$$

$$\frac{9}{10} - \frac{3}{4}$$

$$\frac{5}{16} - \frac{1}{4}$$

$$\frac{3}{5} - \frac{1}{6}$$

$$\frac{5}{6} - \frac{3}{4}$$

$$\frac{2}{3} - \frac{3}{5}$$

$$\frac{1}{6} - \frac{1}{18}$$

$$\frac{11}{14} - \frac{2}{7}$$

$$\frac{1}{2} - \frac{4}{9}$$

$$\frac{4}{9} - \frac{1}{4}$$

$$\frac{11}{15} - \frac{3}{10}$$

$$\frac{3}{4} - \frac{1}{6}$$

11

Fraction Subtraction

unlike denominators

Reduce to Lowest Terms when necessary.

$$\frac{5}{6} - \frac{5}{8}$$ $$\frac{7}{12} - \frac{2}{9}$$ $$\frac{3}{4} - \frac{7}{10}$$ $$\frac{5}{6} - \frac{5}{12}$$

$$\frac{3}{4} - \frac{4}{9}$$ $$\frac{1}{3} - \frac{2}{15}$$ $$\frac{3}{7} - \frac{1}{3}$$ $$\frac{15}{16} - \frac{3}{4}$$

$$\frac{4}{5} - \frac{1}{2}$$ $$\frac{3}{4} - \frac{1}{6}$$ $$\frac{7}{8} - \frac{7}{12}$$ $$\frac{9}{10} - \frac{1}{6}$$

$$\frac{2}{5} - \frac{1}{4}$$ $$\frac{8}{15} - \frac{2}{5}$$ $$\frac{7}{9} - \frac{1}{2}$$ $$\frac{2}{3} - \frac{7}{12}$$

$$\frac{13}{15} - \frac{7}{10}$$ $$\frac{11}{12} - \frac{5}{6}$$ $$\frac{5}{8} - \frac{3}{5}$$ $$\frac{5}{6} - \frac{4}{7}$$

$$\frac{5}{7} - \frac{1}{3}$$ $$\frac{1}{2} - \frac{3}{7}$$ $$\frac{3}{4} - \frac{1}{7}$$ $$\frac{13}{16} - \frac{3}{4}$$

Fraction Subtraction

fractions, mixed numbers, and whole numbers

Reduce to Lowest Terms when necessary.

$$15 \\ -\ 4\frac{2}{5}$$
$$8\frac{7}{10} \\ -\ \frac{1}{2}$$
$$17\frac{15}{16} \\ -\ 9$$
$$3\frac{2}{7} \\ -\ 2\frac{1}{2}$$

$$12\frac{1}{8} \\ -\ 7\frac{3}{4}$$
$$21 \\ -17\frac{1}{2}$$
$$9\frac{3}{4} \\ -\ 6\frac{1}{3}$$
$$14\frac{7}{8} \\ -\ 7$$

$$10\frac{2}{3} \\ -\ \frac{7}{8}$$
$$12\frac{5}{6} \\ -\ 7\frac{5}{12}$$
$$24 \\ -23\frac{11}{12}$$
$$17\frac{2}{5} \\ -\ 6$$

$$4\frac{1}{8} \\ -\ \frac{1}{6}$$
$$8\frac{9}{10} \\ -\ 2\frac{2}{5}$$
$$11\frac{7}{8} \\ -\ \frac{3}{4}$$
$$17 \\ -\ \frac{5}{7}$$

$$14\frac{11}{12} \\ -\ 7$$
$$5\frac{1}{16} \\ -\ 4\frac{3}{4}$$
$$23\frac{1}{7} \\ -15\frac{2}{3}$$
$$7\frac{5}{12} \\ -\ \frac{2}{3}$$

$$12\frac{7}{12} \\ -\ 7\frac{5}{8}$$
$$27 \\ -\ 2\frac{15}{16}$$
$$8\frac{3}{5} \\ -\ 6\frac{3}{4}$$
$$14\frac{1}{6} \\ -\ 9\frac{5}{9}$$

Fraction Subtraction

mixed & whole numbers

Reduce to Lowest Terms when necessary.

$$5\frac{3}{10} - 1\frac{1}{2}$$

$$12\frac{4}{9} - \frac{1}{3}$$

$$9\frac{1}{15} - 4\frac{1}{6}$$

$$11\frac{1}{5} - 7\frac{1}{3}$$

$$6\frac{1}{2} - 5\frac{3}{4}$$

$$27\frac{15}{16} - 13$$

$$8\frac{1}{3} - 4\frac{11}{15}$$

$$3\frac{5}{6} - 2\frac{1}{2}$$

$$24\frac{3}{8} - 15\frac{1}{6}$$

$$15\frac{2}{3} - 12\frac{5}{12}$$

$$7 - 6\frac{7}{17}$$

$$29\frac{5}{8} - 23\frac{7}{16}$$

$$6\frac{1}{12} - 5\frac{5}{8}$$

$$20\frac{1}{6} - 9\frac{1}{7}$$

$$9\frac{3}{4} - 5\frac{15}{16}$$

$$18\frac{1}{4} - 9\frac{1}{6}$$

$$28\frac{1}{5} - 14\frac{7}{10}$$

$$10\frac{3}{8} - 4\frac{3}{4}$$

$$15\frac{1}{2} - 12\frac{5}{8}$$

$$32\frac{1}{2} - 31$$

$$17\frac{1}{6} - 12\frac{3}{5}$$

$$42\frac{1}{2} - 16\frac{2}{3}$$

$$8\frac{1}{2} - 7\frac{1}{3}$$

$$19\frac{7}{8} - 8\frac{11}{16}$$

subtraction

Reduce to Lowest Terms when necessary.

$\frac{7}{9} - \frac{4}{9} =$ $\frac{11}{15} - \frac{8}{15} =$ $\frac{3}{4} - \frac{1}{4} =$ $\frac{9}{14} - \frac{5}{14} =$ $\frac{8}{9} - \frac{4}{9} =$

$$\begin{array}{r} \frac{7}{8} \\ -\frac{5}{8} \end{array} \qquad \begin{array}{r} \frac{15}{16} \\ -\frac{7}{16} \end{array} \qquad \begin{array}{r} \frac{17}{20} \\ -\frac{9}{20} \end{array} \qquad \begin{array}{r} \frac{11}{12} \\ -\frac{3}{12} \end{array} \qquad \begin{array}{r} \frac{5}{11} \\ -\frac{3}{11} \end{array}$$

$$\begin{array}{r} \frac{1}{2} \\ -\frac{1}{4} \end{array} \qquad \begin{array}{r} \frac{5}{6} \\ -\frac{3}{4} \end{array} \qquad \begin{array}{r} \frac{1}{3} \\ -\frac{2}{15} \end{array} \qquad \begin{array}{r} \frac{2}{5} \\ -\frac{1}{4} \end{array} \qquad \begin{array}{r} \frac{11}{14} \\ -\frac{2}{7} \end{array}$$

$$\begin{array}{r} \frac{1}{2} \\ -\frac{3}{7} \end{array} \qquad \begin{array}{r} \frac{7}{9} \\ -\frac{1}{2} \end{array} \qquad \begin{array}{r} \frac{6}{7} \\ -\frac{1}{3} \end{array} \qquad \begin{array}{r} \frac{11}{12} \\ -\frac{5}{6} \end{array} \qquad \begin{array}{r} \frac{2}{3} \\ -\frac{5}{12} \end{array}$$

$$\begin{array}{r} 22 \\ -15\frac{1}{2} \end{array} \qquad \begin{array}{r} 11\frac{5}{6} \\ -7\frac{5}{12} \end{array} \qquad \begin{array}{r} 23\frac{6}{7} \\ -14\frac{2}{3} \end{array} \qquad \begin{array}{r} 9\frac{3}{4} \\ -6\frac{1}{3} \end{array}$$

$$\begin{array}{r} 28\frac{3}{5} \\ -16\frac{9}{10} \end{array} \qquad \begin{array}{r} 37\frac{3}{8} \\ -5\frac{3}{4} \end{array} \qquad \begin{array}{r} 8\frac{1}{3} \\ -7\frac{1}{2} \end{array} \qquad \begin{array}{r} 18\frac{4}{9} \\ -\frac{2}{3} \end{array}$$

Fraction Multiplication

fractions × fractions

Reduce to Lowest Terms when necessary.

$\frac{1}{2} \times \frac{1}{3} =$ $\frac{1}{4} \times \frac{1}{2} =$ $\frac{2}{3} \times \frac{3}{4} =$ $\frac{1}{5} \times \frac{1}{3} =$

$\frac{4}{5} \times \frac{2}{3} =$ $\frac{3}{5} \times \frac{4}{7} =$ $\frac{1}{4} \times \frac{1}{3} =$ $\frac{1}{2} \times \frac{4}{9} =$

$\frac{3}{4} \times \frac{2}{7} =$ $\frac{9}{10} \times \frac{2}{3} =$ $\frac{3}{4} \times \frac{4}{5} =$ $\frac{1}{5} \times \frac{1}{2} =$

$\frac{3}{8} \times \frac{5}{8} =$ $\frac{2}{5} \times \frac{5}{8} =$ $\frac{7}{10} \times \frac{5}{6} =$ $\frac{6}{7} \times \frac{5}{6} =$

$\frac{3}{4} \times \frac{8}{9} =$ $\frac{1}{12} \times \frac{3}{5} =$ $\frac{1}{3} \times \frac{9}{10} =$ $\frac{1}{4} \times \frac{8}{9} =$

$\frac{3}{7} \times \frac{1}{3} =$ $\frac{4}{5} \times \frac{2}{7} =$ $\frac{7}{20} \times \frac{3}{5} =$ $\frac{3}{8} \times \frac{1}{2} =$

Fraction Multiplication

fractions × fractions

Reduce to Lowest Terms when necessary.

$\frac{4}{5} \times \frac{15}{16} =$ $\frac{1}{2} \times \frac{13}{14} =$ $\frac{7}{10} \times \frac{2}{3} =$ $\frac{3}{4} \times \frac{3}{7} =$

$\frac{4}{5} \times \frac{3}{12} =$ $\frac{7}{9} \times \frac{3}{7} =$ $\frac{1}{3} \times \frac{3}{4} =$ $\frac{3}{7} \times \frac{5}{7} =$

$\frac{5}{6} \times \frac{3}{5} =$ $\frac{4}{5} \times \frac{11}{5} =$ $\frac{1}{12} \times \frac{4}{5} =$ $\frac{5}{6} \times \frac{2}{7} =$

$\frac{9}{12} \times \frac{3}{4} =$ $\frac{1}{4} \times \frac{6}{11} =$ $\frac{4}{11} \times \frac{3}{16} =$ $\frac{3}{8} \times \frac{1}{9} =$

$\frac{1}{2} \times \frac{6}{5} =$ $\frac{6}{11} \times \frac{3}{4} =$ $\frac{5}{6} \times \frac{9}{10} =$ $\frac{6}{8} \times \frac{12}{4} =$

$\frac{1}{4} \times \frac{3}{16} =$ $\frac{4}{5} \times \frac{1}{2} =$ $\frac{4}{5} \times \frac{5}{7} =$ $\frac{5}{9} \times \frac{8}{5} =$

Fraction Multiplication

fractions, mixed numbers, and whole numbers

Reduce to Lowest Terms when necessary.

$\frac{3}{5} \times 5 =$ $6 \times \frac{7}{8} =$ $\frac{3}{5} \times \frac{4}{15} =$ $\frac{3}{7} \times 28 =$

$\frac{14}{15} \times \frac{5}{7} =$ $\frac{4}{9} \times 63 =$ $24 \times \frac{11}{12} =$ $\frac{7}{8} \times 96 =$

$1\frac{1}{2} \times 5 =$ $3\frac{2}{7} \times 4 =$ $10 \times 5\frac{3}{4} =$ $3\frac{3}{4} \times \frac{1}{2} =$

$\frac{7}{8} \times 5\frac{11}{12} =$ $15 \times \frac{5}{6} =$ $1\frac{1}{3} \times 1\frac{1}{3} =$ $2\frac{3}{4} \times \frac{5}{6} =$

$3\frac{1}{5} \times 2\frac{2}{3} =$ $\frac{5}{8} \times 12 =$ $3\frac{1}{2} \times \frac{4}{9} =$ $1\frac{1}{2} \times 2\frac{3}{8} =$

$6\frac{3}{8} \times 2\frac{2}{5} =$ $3\frac{3}{5} \times 2\frac{5}{6} =$ $4\frac{2}{3} \times 4\frac{3}{8} =$ $2\frac{3}{10} \times 1\frac{1}{2} =$

Fraction Multiplication

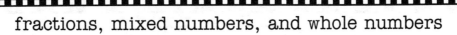

fractions, mixed numbers, and whole numbers

Reduce to Lowest Terms when necessary.

$5\frac{1}{4} \times \frac{2}{9} =$ $2\frac{1}{4} \times 2\frac{2}{3} =$ $4\frac{1}{2} \times 7\frac{1}{3} =$ $2\frac{2}{7} \times 2\frac{5}{8} =$

$3\frac{7}{8} \times 24 =$ $4\frac{1}{8} \times 5\frac{1}{3} =$ $10 \times 10\frac{1}{10} =$ $2\frac{1}{4} \times 2\frac{7}{12} =$

$\frac{2}{3} \times 2\frac{11}{12} =$ $4\frac{1}{6} \times 2\frac{2}{5} =$ $7\frac{1}{2} \times 6\frac{1}{15} =$ $3\frac{1}{8} \times 4\frac{3}{5} =$

$2\frac{2}{7} \times 2\frac{7}{8} =$ $\frac{6}{7} \times \frac{24}{1} =$ $5\frac{2}{5} \times 7\frac{1}{3} =$ $\frac{15}{16} \times 1\frac{1}{3} =$

$3\frac{3}{4} \times 3\frac{1}{6} =$ $\frac{1}{2} \times 20\frac{1}{4} =$ $6\frac{3}{7} \times 6\frac{1}{5} =$ $6\frac{1}{2} \times \frac{5}{6} =$

$8\frac{1}{2} \times 1\frac{1}{4} =$ $\frac{1}{18} \times 6\frac{2}{5} =$ $3\frac{1}{10} \times 5\frac{1}{2} =$ $6\frac{1}{2} \times 24 =$

Section Diagnostic Test

multiplication

Reduce to Lowest Terms when necessary.

$\frac{1}{3} \times \frac{1}{2} =$ $\frac{3}{8} \times \frac{1}{2} =$ $\frac{9}{10} \times \frac{3}{5} =$ $\frac{5}{6} \times \frac{7}{8} =$

$\frac{2}{3} \times \frac{3}{4} =$ $\frac{15}{16} \times \frac{2}{3} =$ $\frac{1}{12} \times \frac{4}{5} =$ $\frac{6}{7} \times \frac{5}{6} =$

$\frac{2}{5} \times 50 =$ $12 \times \frac{9}{12} =$ $4 \times \frac{11}{12} =$ $\frac{2}{15} \times 15 =$

$5\frac{1}{4} \times \frac{2}{9} =$ $3\frac{1}{2} \times \frac{4}{9} =$ $\frac{5}{8} \times 3\frac{1}{2} =$ $\frac{3}{4} \times 6\frac{11}{12} =$

$6\frac{3}{8} \times 2\frac{2}{5} =$ $1\frac{1}{2} \times 2\frac{3}{8} =$ $4\frac{1}{8} \times 5\frac{1}{3} =$ $8\frac{1}{2} \times 1\frac{1}{4} =$

$6\frac{3}{7} \times 6\frac{1}{5} =$ $3\frac{1}{10} \times 5\frac{1}{2} =$ $2\frac{2}{7} \times 2\frac{7}{8} =$ $12\frac{1}{3} \times 2\frac{3}{5} =$

20

Fraction Division

fractions ÷ fractions

Reduce to Lowest Terms when necessary.

$\frac{1}{4} \div \frac{1}{2} =$ $\frac{3}{4} \div \frac{1}{2} =$ $\frac{1}{4} \div \frac{1}{8} =$ $\frac{1}{3} \div \frac{3}{4} =$

$\frac{1}{6} \div \frac{1}{8} =$ $\frac{2}{3} \div \frac{3}{4} =$ $\frac{1}{4} \div \frac{1}{4} =$ $\frac{1}{8} \div \frac{1}{4} =$

$\frac{4}{5} \div \frac{3}{4} =$ $\frac{1}{2} \div \frac{1}{3} =$ $\frac{1}{5} \div \frac{1}{4} =$ $\frac{3}{8} \div \frac{1}{2} =$

$\frac{4}{7} \div \frac{3}{4} =$ $\frac{1}{6} \div \frac{1}{2} =$ $\frac{2}{3} \div \frac{2}{5} =$ $\frac{5}{8} \div \frac{5}{6} =$

$\frac{1}{2} \div \frac{1}{2} =$ $\frac{4}{5} \div \frac{8}{9} =$ $\frac{1}{4} \div \frac{3}{4} =$ $\frac{1}{8} \div \frac{7}{8} =$

$\frac{3}{4} \div \frac{3}{8} =$ $\frac{5}{6} \div \frac{2}{7} =$ $\frac{1}{3} \div \frac{2}{3} =$ $\frac{1}{10} \div \frac{2}{5} =$

21

Fraction Division

fractions ÷ fractions

Reduce to Lowest Terms when necessary.

$\frac{3}{8} \div \frac{3}{4} =$ $\frac{1}{4} \div \frac{5}{6} =$ $\frac{9}{10} \div \frac{3}{5} =$ $\frac{2}{3} \div \frac{5}{9} =$

$\frac{1}{6} \div \frac{5}{12} =$ $\frac{5}{9} \div \frac{1}{7} =$ $\frac{3}{8} \div \frac{7}{12} =$ $\frac{3}{8} \div \frac{4}{15} =$

$\frac{3}{4} \div \frac{3}{5} =$ $\frac{5}{6} \div \frac{1}{2} =$ $\frac{5}{8} \div \frac{1}{4} =$ $\frac{2}{5} \div \frac{15}{16} =$

$\frac{6}{7} \div \frac{5}{21} =$ $\frac{4}{7} \div \frac{3}{7} =$ $\frac{7}{10} \div \frac{3}{4} =$ $\frac{2}{3} \div \frac{4}{5} =$

$\frac{1}{12} \div \frac{3}{8} =$ $\frac{3}{5} \div \frac{1}{3} =$ $\frac{5}{16} \div \frac{3}{8} =$ $\frac{11}{12} \div \frac{5}{6} =$

$\frac{3}{5} \div \frac{9}{10} =$ $\frac{5}{6} \div \frac{7}{9} =$ $\frac{13}{20} \div \frac{1}{2} =$ $\frac{8}{9} \div \frac{4}{5} =$

Fraction Division

mixed & whole numbers ÷ fractions

Reduce to Lowest Terms when necessary.

$\frac{1}{2} \div 2 =$ $8 \div \frac{1}{10} =$ $1\frac{1}{2} \div 5 =$ $2\frac{1}{4} \div \frac{1}{2} =$

$2\frac{1}{8} \div 17 =$ $\frac{1}{2} \div 3\frac{1}{3} =$ $1\frac{7}{10} \div \frac{4}{5} =$ $3\frac{1}{2} \div 14 =$

$\frac{3}{16} \div 3 =$ $\frac{3}{4} \div 4\frac{1}{8} =$ $2\frac{1}{2} \div 1\frac{1}{4} =$ $3\frac{3}{8} \div \frac{1}{4} =$

$3 \div \frac{3}{8} =$ $4\frac{2}{3} \div \frac{7}{8} =$ $1\frac{5}{8} \div 1\frac{1}{4} =$ $7\frac{1}{3} \div 11 =$

$3\frac{1}{2} \div 4\frac{1}{2} =$ $6\frac{3}{10} \div 2\frac{1}{5} =$ $5\frac{1}{2} \div 1\frac{5}{6} =$ $4\frac{1}{3} \div 26 =$

$2\frac{1}{7} \div 1\frac{2}{3} =$ $12\frac{1}{2} \div 6\frac{1}{4} =$ $2\frac{1}{4} \div 1\frac{1}{2} =$ $14 \div 14\frac{1}{2} =$

Fraction Division

mixed numbers ÷ mixed numbers

Reduce to Lowest Terms when necessary.

$5\frac{1}{4} \div 2\frac{1}{3} =$ $\qquad$ $8\frac{3}{4} \div 5\frac{2}{5} =$ $\qquad$ $1\frac{1}{6} \div 2\frac{11}{12} =$ $\qquad$ $1\frac{4}{9} \div 2\frac{1}{2} =$

$3\frac{1}{4} \div 2\frac{1}{2} =$ $\qquad$ $1\frac{1}{10} \div 2\frac{1}{7} =$ $\qquad$ $3\frac{1}{5} \div 2\frac{2}{7} =$ $\qquad$ $12\frac{1}{2} \div 4\frac{1}{8} =$

$3\frac{1}{7} \div 2\frac{1}{14} =$ $\qquad$ $10\frac{1}{8} \div 1\frac{1}{2} =$ $\qquad$ $4\frac{1}{15} \div 3\frac{1}{5} =$ $\qquad$ $6\frac{1}{9} \div 5\frac{1}{2} =$

$2\frac{3}{4} \div 5\frac{1}{4} =$ $\qquad$ $5\frac{5}{6} \div 4\frac{2}{3} =$ $\qquad$ $8\frac{2}{3} \div 10\frac{1}{2} =$ $\qquad$ $1\frac{1}{14} \div 2\frac{1}{12} =$

$5\frac{1}{3} \div 4\frac{7}{8} =$ $\qquad$ $25\frac{1}{2} \div 5\frac{5}{6} =$ $\qquad$ $8\frac{3}{4} \div 1\frac{3}{4} =$ $\qquad$ $2\frac{7}{8} \div 3\frac{5}{6} =$

$6\frac{1}{3} \div 4\frac{5}{12} =$ $\qquad$ $7\frac{2}{5} \div 5\frac{2}{3} =$ $\qquad$ $8\frac{2}{3} \div 6\frac{1}{2} =$ $\qquad$ $3\frac{1}{10} \div 4\frac{3}{10} =$

division

Reduce to Lowest Terms when necessary.

$\frac{1}{6} \div \frac{1}{8} =$ $\qquad$ $\frac{1}{2} \div \frac{1}{3} =$ $\qquad$ $\frac{1}{10} \div \frac{2}{5} =$ $\qquad$ $\frac{1}{3} \div \frac{3}{4} =$

$8 \div \frac{1}{10} =$ $\qquad$ $1\frac{7}{10} \div \frac{4}{5} =$ $\qquad$ $\frac{3}{4} \div 4\frac{1}{8} =$ $\qquad$ $1\frac{1}{2} \div 5 =$

$3\frac{1}{2} \div 14 =$ $\qquad$ $1\frac{5}{8} \div 1\frac{1}{4} =$ $\qquad$ $\frac{1}{2} \div 10 =$ $\qquad$ $7\frac{1}{3} \div 11 =$

$10\frac{1}{8} \div 1\frac{1}{2} =$ $\qquad$ $1\frac{4}{9} \div 2\frac{1}{2} =$ $\qquad$ $3\frac{1}{4} \div 2\frac{1}{2} =$ $\qquad$ $7\frac{2}{5} \div 5\frac{2}{3} =$

$6\frac{1}{3} \div 4\frac{5}{12} =$ $\qquad$ $1\frac{1}{6} \div 2\frac{11}{12} =$ $\qquad$ $8\frac{2}{3} \div 6\frac{1}{2} =$ $\qquad$ $3\frac{1}{10} \div 4\frac{3}{10} =$

Review Sheet

Reduce to Lowest Terms when necessary.

$2\frac{3}{8} + 3\frac{3}{8} =$ $\qquad$ $\frac{9}{10} - \frac{3}{10} =$ $\qquad$ $\frac{3}{4} \times \frac{2}{7} =$ $\qquad$ $\frac{1}{3} \div \frac{3}{4} =$

$$\begin{array}{r} \frac{2}{3} \\ + \frac{3}{4} \\ \hline \end{array} \qquad \begin{array}{r} \frac{1}{2} \\ + \frac{1}{9} \\ \hline \end{array} \qquad \begin{array}{r} 10\frac{1}{3} \\ + 4\frac{5}{7} \\ \hline \end{array} \qquad \begin{array}{r} 24\frac{7}{10} \\ +19\frac{3}{4} \\ \hline \end{array} \qquad \begin{array}{r} 10\frac{5}{12} \\ + 4\frac{7}{8} \\ \hline \end{array}$$

$$\begin{array}{r} \frac{9}{10} \\ - \frac{3}{4} \\ \hline \end{array} \qquad \begin{array}{r} \frac{3}{5} \\ - \frac{1}{6} \\ \hline \end{array} \qquad \begin{array}{r} 27 \\ - 5\frac{5}{16} \\ \hline \end{array} \qquad \begin{array}{r} 8\frac{3}{5} \\ - 6\frac{3}{4} \\ \hline \end{array} \qquad \begin{array}{r} 19\frac{7}{8} \\ - 8\frac{11}{16} \\ \hline \end{array}$$

$\frac{6}{11} \times \frac{3}{4} =$ $\qquad$ $\frac{1}{2} \times 20\frac{1}{4} =$ $\qquad$ $5\frac{1}{4} \times \frac{2}{9} =$ $\qquad$ $\frac{5}{8} \times 12 =$

$2\frac{2}{7} \times 2\frac{7}{8} =$ $\qquad$ $4\frac{1}{6} \times 2\frac{2}{5} =$ $\qquad$ $1\frac{1}{3} \times 1\frac{1}{3} =$ $\qquad$ $10 \times 5\frac{3}{4} =$

$\frac{3}{4} \div \frac{3}{8} =$ $\qquad$ $\frac{4}{5} \div \frac{8}{9} =$ $\qquad$ $\frac{1}{4} \div \frac{3}{4} =$ $\qquad$ $\frac{2}{5} \div \frac{15}{16} =$

$\frac{1}{2} \div 2 =$ $\qquad$ $1\frac{5}{8} \div 1\frac{1}{4} =$ $\qquad$ $3\frac{1}{4} \div 2\frac{1}{2} =$ $\qquad$ $1\frac{1}{6} \div 2\frac{11}{12} =$

Final Assessment Test

Reduce all answers to lowest terms.

$1\frac{3}{4} + 1\frac{3}{4} =$

$$12\frac{1}{3}$$
$$+ \ 7\frac{7}{15}$$

$$\frac{2}{3}$$
$$+ \ \ \frac{1}{7}$$

$$4\frac{3}{5}$$
$$+ \ 2\frac{1}{6}$$

$$9\frac{3}{5}$$
$$+ \ 1\frac{1}{8}$$

$\frac{15}{16} + \frac{15}{16} =$

$\frac{15}{16} - \frac{9}{16} =$

$$\frac{4}{5}$$
$$- \ \frac{1}{2}$$

$$\frac{7}{8}$$
$$- \ \frac{7}{12}$$

$$23\frac{1}{7}$$
$$-15\frac{2}{3}$$

$$10\frac{3}{8}$$
$$- \ 4\frac{3}{4}$$

$\frac{3}{4} - \frac{1}{4} =$

$\frac{2}{3} \times \frac{3}{4} =$

$1\frac{1}{3} \times 1\frac{1}{3} =$

$3\frac{3}{4} \times \frac{1}{2} =$

$\frac{3}{7} \times 28 =$

$\frac{4}{5} \times \frac{15}{16} =$

$\frac{1}{2} \times 20\frac{1}{4} =$

$3\frac{3}{5} \times 2\frac{5}{6} =$

$2\frac{3}{10} \times 1\frac{1}{2} =$

$\frac{3}{4} \div \frac{1}{2} =$

$\frac{1}{2} \div \frac{1}{3} =$

$\frac{11}{12} \div \frac{5}{6} =$

$\frac{5}{9} \div \frac{1}{7} =$

$8 \div \frac{1}{10} =$

$\frac{3}{4} \div 4\frac{1}{8} =$

$5\frac{1}{4} \div 2\frac{1}{3} =$

$1\frac{4}{9} \div 2\frac{1}{2} =$

Answers

Beginning Assessment Test, page 1.

The **Beginning Assessment Test** is arranged horizontally by skills. This arrangement will identify skills which are firm and skills which need attention. Note that answers for equivalent fractions may vary.

Basic Concepts

$\frac{1}{2} = \frac{2}{4}$ $\frac{5}{10} = \frac{1}{2}$ $\frac{5}{4} = 1\frac{1}{4}$ $2\frac{1}{2} = \frac{5}{2}$

$\frac{1}{5} = \frac{2}{10}$ $\frac{4}{6} = \frac{2}{3}$ $\frac{10}{7} = 1\frac{3}{7}$ $6\frac{1}{8} = \frac{49}{8}$

$\frac{3}{4} = \frac{6}{8}$ $\frac{16}{20} = \frac{4}{5}$ $\frac{20}{12} = 1\frac{2}{3}$ $4\frac{3}{15} = \frac{63}{15}$

$\frac{1}{3} = \frac{3}{9}$ $\frac{3}{12} = \frac{1}{4}$ $\frac{14}{4} = 3\frac{1}{2}$ $5\frac{7}{8} = \frac{47}{8}$

Addition

$\begin{array}{r} \frac{3}{4} \\ +\ \frac{3}{4} \\ \hline 1\frac{1}{2} \end{array}$

$\frac{1}{8} + \frac{4}{8} = \frac{5}{8}$
$\frac{1}{8} + \frac{1}{2} = \frac{5}{8}$

$\begin{array}{r} 8\frac{1}{2} \\ +\ 4\frac{1}{6} \\ \hline 12\frac{2}{3} \end{array}$

$\frac{1}{3} + \frac{1}{6} = \frac{1}{2}$
$2\frac{3}{8} + 2\frac{3}{8} = 4\frac{3}{4}$

$\begin{array}{r} 24\frac{1}{2} \\ +17\frac{2}{3} \\ \hline 42\frac{1}{6} \end{array}$

Subtraction

$\frac{2}{3} - \frac{2}{3} = 0$
$\frac{8}{9} - \frac{4}{9} = \frac{4}{9}$

$\begin{array}{r} \frac{1}{2} \\ -\ \frac{1}{4} \\ \hline \frac{1}{4} \end{array}$

$\begin{array}{r} \frac{3}{8} \\ -\ \frac{1}{4} \\ \hline \frac{1}{8} \end{array}$

$\begin{array}{r} 15 \\ -\ 4\frac{2}{5} \\ \hline 10\frac{3}{5} \end{array}$

$\begin{array}{r} 10\frac{3}{8} \\ -\ 4\frac{3}{4} \\ \hline 5\frac{5}{8} \end{array}$

Multiplication

$\frac{1}{2} \times \frac{1}{3} = \frac{1}{6}$ $\frac{3}{5} \times 5 = 3$ $5\frac{1}{4} \times \frac{2}{9} = 1\frac{1}{6}$ $4\frac{1}{6} \times 2\frac{2}{5} = 10$

Division

$\frac{1}{4} \div \frac{1}{2} = \frac{1}{2}$ $\frac{3}{8} \div \frac{3}{4} = \frac{1}{2}$ $1\frac{5}{8} \div 1\frac{1}{4} = 1\frac{3}{10}$ $2\frac{1}{2} \div \frac{1}{2} = 5$

PRACTICE SHEET, PAGE 2.

$\frac{2}{4}$	$\frac{3}{24}$	$\frac{4}{18}\ \frac{6}{27}$	$\frac{3}{12}\ \frac{4}{16}\ \frac{5}{20}$		
$\frac{2}{8}$	$\frac{6}{8}$	$\frac{4}{6}\ \frac{6}{9}$	$\frac{9}{12}\ \frac{12}{16}\ \frac{18}{24}$		
$\frac{3}{9}$	$\frac{4}{14}$	$\frac{4}{10}\ \frac{6}{15}$	$\frac{25}{50}\ \frac{50}{100}\ \frac{100}{200}$		
$\frac{2}{10}$	$\frac{22}{24}$	$\frac{10}{12}\ \frac{15}{18}$	$\frac{14}{16}\ \frac{21}{24}\ \frac{28}{32}$	$\frac{8}{10}\ \frac{4}{5}$	$\frac{1}{2}$ $\frac{1}{4}$ $\frac{1}{3}$
$\frac{2}{12}$	$\frac{9}{15}$	$\frac{50}{200}\ \frac{75}{300}$	$\frac{28}{40}\ \frac{35}{50}\ \frac{56}{80}$	$\frac{2}{6}\ \frac{1}{3}$	$\frac{2}{5}$ $\frac{1}{3}$ $\frac{2}{3}$
$\frac{3}{30}$	$\frac{44}{50}$	$\frac{4}{100}\ \frac{6}{150}$	$\frac{150}{300}\ \frac{200}{400}\ \frac{500}{1000}$	$\frac{6}{8}\ \frac{3}{4}$	$\frac{8}{9}$ $\frac{4}{9}$ $\frac{1}{4}$
				$\frac{1}{2}$	$\frac{2}{3}$ $\frac{2}{3}$ $\frac{5}{8}$
				$\frac{2}{3}$	$\frac{3}{5}$ $\frac{3}{5}$ $\frac{1}{3}$
				$\frac{9}{10}$	$\frac{8}{17}$ $\frac{7}{8}$ $\frac{5}{7}$
				$\frac{1}{4}$	$\frac{3}{7}$ $\frac{1}{4}$ $\frac{5}{21}$

PRACTICE SHEET, PAGE 3.

$1\frac{1}{3}$	$4\frac{2}{3}$	$9\frac{3}{5}$	$4\frac{1}{4}$
2	$3\frac{1}{2}$	$7\frac{1}{2}$	$3\frac{1}{2}$
$1\frac{3}{5}$	$1\frac{2}{3}$	$6\frac{2}{11}$	$3\frac{9}{10}$
$5\frac{1}{2}$	$1\frac{2}{3}$	$2\frac{5}{12}$	$5\frac{2}{5}$
$1\frac{3}{7}$	$3\frac{1}{7}$	$2\frac{1}{27}$	$9\frac{1}{3}$
$2\frac{1}{4}$	$1\frac{1}{3}$	$4\frac{7}{9}$	$7\frac{5}{6}$
1	$2\frac{1}{4}$	$3\frac{1}{33}$	$2\frac{1}{2}$
$1\frac{1}{4}$	$1\frac{5}{8}$	3	12

continued on next page

Answers

PRACTICE SHEET, PAGE 4.

$\frac{5}{2}$	$\frac{51}{16}$	$\frac{59}{8}$	$\frac{19}{4}$
$\frac{13}{3}$	$\frac{53}{9}$	$\frac{26}{3}$	$\frac{79}{11}$
$\frac{23}{4}$	$\frac{53}{12}$	$\frac{61}{12}$	$\frac{51}{16}$
$\frac{39}{10}$	$\frac{37}{4}$	$\frac{27}{7}$	$\frac{17}{3}$
$\frac{49}{8}$	$\frac{47}{15}$	$\frac{63}{15}$	$\frac{47}{8}$
$\frac{37}{5}$	$\frac{41}{6}$	$\frac{34}{5}$	$\frac{69}{7}$
$\frac{5}{3}$	$\frac{35}{12}$	$\frac{40}{9}$	$\frac{35}{12}$
$\frac{17}{7}$	$\frac{17}{2}$	$\frac{67}{10}$	$\frac{64}{9}$

$\frac{1}{2}$	$\frac{5}{8}$	$\frac{4}{5}$	$\frac{11}{12}$	$\frac{4}{5}$	
1	$\frac{3}{4}$	$\frac{8}{11}$	$1\frac{1}{6}$	$1\frac{1}{2}$	
$\frac{8}{9}$	$\frac{2}{3}$	$1\frac{1}{8}$	$\frac{6}{7}$	$\frac{3}{4}$	
$\frac{7}{8}$	$1\frac{1}{10}$	1	$1\frac{3}{4}$	$\frac{2}{3}$	
$3\frac{1}{2}$	$1\frac{7}{8}$	$2\frac{4}{11}$	$5\frac{3}{4}$	$1\frac{5}{6}$	
$1\frac{1}{2}$	$1\frac{1}{2}$	2	$1\frac{1}{11}$	$1\frac{1}{5}$	$\frac{3}{4}$
$3\frac{7}{15}$	1	$6\frac{2}{3}$	$1\frac{9}{10}$	$1\frac{1}{9}$	$4\frac{4}{5}$
$9\frac{15}{16}$	$4\frac{14}{15}$	$\frac{19}{20}$	$10\frac{3}{7}$	$1\frac{3}{4}$	$8\frac{1}{16}$

PRACTICE SHEET, PAGE 5.

$\frac{3}{4}$	$\frac{1}{2}$	$\frac{5}{8}$	$\frac{7}{10}$
$\frac{5}{8}$	$\frac{8}{9}$	$\frac{2}{3}$	$\frac{7}{8}$
$\frac{11}{12}$	$\frac{9}{10}$	$1\frac{1}{10}$	$1\frac{1}{8}$
$\frac{11}{14}$	$\frac{11}{12}$	$1\frac{1}{15}$	$\frac{17}{18}$
$1\frac{4}{15}$	1	$\frac{8}{9}$	$1\frac{1}{6}$
$1\frac{7}{12}$	$\frac{13}{21}$	$\frac{19}{24}$	$\frac{23}{30}$

PRACTICE SHEET, PAGE 6.

$1\frac{11}{24}$	$\frac{29}{36}$	$\frac{11}{20}$	$1\frac{1}{3}$
$1\frac{11}{36}$	$1\frac{1}{6}$	$\frac{13}{14}$	$1\frac{17}{42}$
$\frac{17}{21}$	$\frac{1}{2}$	$\frac{41}{72}$	$1\frac{7}{20}$
$1\frac{1}{8}$	$1\frac{2}{3}$	$1\frac{2}{3}$	$1\frac{7}{18}$
$2\frac{2}{15}$	$\frac{19}{24}$	$\frac{13}{15}$	$1\frac{19}{28}$

PRACTICE SHEET, PAGE 7.

$12\frac{2}{3}$	$18\frac{1}{5}$	$12\frac{7}{9}$	$12\frac{3}{7}$
$18\frac{25}{28}$	$88\frac{5}{12}$	$40\frac{9}{10}$	$20\frac{3}{4}$
$15\frac{11}{20}$	$19\frac{4}{5}$	$42\frac{7}{8}$	$17\frac{11}{18}$
$51\frac{11}{12}$	$31\frac{1}{21}$	$73\frac{2}{7}$	$20\frac{5}{6}$
$26\frac{13}{20}$	$35\frac{11}{12}$	$31\frac{17}{24}$	$22\frac{5}{12}$
$15\frac{1}{3}$	$40\frac{29}{40}$	$60\frac{7}{15}$	$22\frac{11}{12}$

PRACTICE SHEET, PAGE 8.

$90\frac{7}{8}$	$45\frac{5}{24}$	$42\frac{1}{6}$	$38\frac{7}{20}$
$49\frac{7}{24}$	$41\frac{17}{18}$	$43\frac{7}{16}$	$85\frac{5}{42}$
$53\frac{2}{5}$	$36\frac{1}{21}$	$86\frac{23}{30}$	$69\frac{32}{33}$
$107\frac{21}{40}$	$42\frac{17}{30}$	$36\frac{1}{6}$	$48\frac{1}{28}$
$64\frac{11}{18}$	$77\frac{23}{24}$	$58\frac{7}{24}$	$42\frac{3}{8}$
$51\frac{9}{20}$	$53\frac{1}{10}$	$112\frac{7}{16}$	$13\frac{3}{4}$

PRACTICE SHEET, PAGE 10.

$\frac{1}{3}$	$\frac{2}{5}$	$\frac{3}{7}$	$\frac{1}{2}$	$\frac{1}{10}$
$\frac{3}{11}$	$\frac{4}{9}$	$\frac{2}{3}$	$\frac{1}{2}$	$\frac{1}{7}$
0	$\frac{1}{19}$	$\frac{1}{3}$	$\frac{3}{7}$	$\frac{1}{3}$
$\frac{1}{10}$	$\frac{1}{4}$	$\frac{1}{4}$	$\frac{1}{6}$	$\frac{2}{9}$
$\frac{1}{5}$	$\frac{1}{15}$	$\frac{3}{8}$	$\frac{7}{15}$	$\frac{3}{5}$
$\frac{1}{2}$	$\frac{1}{4}$	$\frac{5}{6}$	$\frac{6}{11}$	$\frac{1}{2}$
$\frac{3}{8}$	$\frac{1}{3}$	$\frac{7}{15}$	$\frac{1}{2}$	$\frac{1}{3}$
$\frac{1}{5}$	$\frac{7}{16}$	$\frac{2}{5}$	$\frac{2}{15}$	$\frac{1}{9}$

PRACTICE SHEET, PAGE 11.

$\frac{1}{4}$	$\frac{1}{6}$	$\frac{1}{8}$	$\frac{1}{10}$
$\frac{1}{8}$	$\frac{4}{9}$	0	$\frac{4}{15}$
$\frac{5}{12}$	$\frac{11}{21}$	$\frac{1}{12}$	$\frac{1}{8}$
$\frac{13}{24}$	$\frac{3}{20}$	$\frac{1}{16}$	$\frac{13}{30}$
$\frac{1}{12}$	$\frac{1}{15}$	$\frac{1}{9}$	$\frac{1}{2}$
$\frac{1}{18}$	$\frac{7}{36}$	$\frac{13}{30}$	$\frac{7}{12}$

Answers

Section Diagnostic Test, page 9.

The **Section Diagnostic Tests** are specially arranged too.
The arrangement helps to identify if there are still problems
and for which skills those problems occur.

$\frac{1}{7} + \frac{3}{7} = \frac{4}{7}$ $\frac{5}{10} + \frac{3}{10} = \frac{4}{5}$ $\frac{3}{8} + \frac{5}{8} = 1$ $\frac{5}{6} + \frac{5}{6} = 1\frac{2}{3}$

Like Denominators

$\frac{5}{12} + \frac{1}{12} = \frac{1}{2}$ $\frac{4}{9} + \frac{2}{9} = \frac{2}{3}$ $\frac{7}{16} + \frac{11}{16} = 1\frac{1}{8}$ $\frac{1}{11} + \frac{8}{11} = \frac{9}{11}$

$$\begin{array}{r}\frac{1}{2}\\[2pt]+\ \frac{3}{4}\\\hline 1\frac{1}{4}\end{array} \qquad \begin{array}{r}\frac{1}{3}\\[2pt]+\ \frac{1}{6}\\\hline \frac{1}{2}\end{array} \qquad \begin{array}{r}\frac{5}{12}\\[2pt]+\ \frac{3}{4}\\\hline 1\frac{1}{6}\end{array} \qquad \begin{array}{r}\frac{3}{8}\\[2pt]+\ \frac{1}{4}\\\hline \frac{5}{8}\end{array}$$

Unlike Denominators

$$\begin{array}{r}\frac{1}{6}\\[2pt]+\ \frac{3}{4}\\\hline \frac{11}{12}\end{array} \qquad \begin{array}{r}\frac{1}{4}\\[2pt]+\ \frac{3}{5}\\\hline \frac{17}{20}\end{array} \qquad \begin{array}{r}\frac{7}{10}\\[2pt]+\ \frac{3}{4}\\\hline 1\frac{9}{20}\end{array} \qquad \begin{array}{r}\frac{1}{4}\\[2pt]+\ \frac{5}{6}\\\hline 1\frac{1}{2}\end{array}$$

$$\begin{array}{r}45\frac{1}{2}\\[2pt]+17\frac{2}{5}\\\hline 62\frac{9}{10}\end{array} \qquad \begin{array}{r}23\frac{1}{8}\\[2pt]+12\frac{1}{3}\\\hline 35\frac{11}{24}\end{array} \qquad \begin{array}{r}50\frac{9}{10}\\[2pt]+\ 2\frac{5}{6}\\\hline 53\frac{11}{15}\end{array} \qquad \begin{array}{r}12\frac{3}{7}\\[2pt]+15\frac{1}{6}\\\hline 27\frac{25}{42}\end{array}$$

Mixed & Whole Numbers

$$\begin{array}{r}14\frac{13}{18}\\[2pt]+17\frac{4}{9}\\\hline 32\frac{1}{6}\end{array} \qquad \begin{array}{r}20\frac{1}{2}\\[2pt]+12\frac{3}{7}\\\hline 32\frac{13}{14}\end{array} \qquad \begin{array}{r}86\frac{2}{3}\\[2pt]+12\frac{4}{7}\\\hline 99\frac{5}{21}\end{array} \qquad \begin{array}{r}91\frac{3}{8}\\[2pt]+\ 6\frac{2}{3}\\\hline 98\frac{1}{24}\end{array}$$

PRACTICE SHEET, PAGE 12.				**PRACTICE SHEET, PAGE 13.**				PRACTICE SHEET, PAGE 14.			
$\frac{5}{24}$	$\frac{13}{36}$	$\frac{1}{20}$	$\frac{5}{12}$	$10\frac{3}{5}$	$8\frac{1}{5}$	$8\frac{15}{16}$	$\frac{11}{14}$	$3\frac{4}{5}$	$12\frac{1}{9}$	$4\frac{9}{10}$	$3\frac{13}{15}$
$\frac{11}{36}$	$\frac{1}{5}$	$\frac{2}{21}$	$\frac{3}{16}$	$4\frac{3}{8}$	$3\frac{1}{2}$	$3\frac{5}{12}$	$7\frac{7}{8}$	$\frac{3}{4}$	$14\frac{15}{16}$	$3\frac{3}{5}$	$1\frac{1}{3}$
$\frac{3}{10}$	$\frac{7}{12}$	$\frac{7}{24}$	$\frac{11}{15}$	$9\frac{19}{24}$	$5\frac{5}{12}$	$\frac{1}{12}$	$11\frac{2}{5}$	$9\frac{5}{24}$	$3\frac{1}{4}$	$\frac{10}{17}$	$6\frac{3}{16}$
$\frac{3}{20}$	$\frac{2}{15}$	$\frac{5}{18}$	$\frac{1}{12}$	$3\frac{23}{24}$	$6\frac{1}{2}$	$11\frac{1}{8}$	$16\frac{2}{7}$	$\frac{11}{24}$	$11\frac{1}{42}$	$3\frac{13}{16}$	$9\frac{1}{12}$
$\frac{1}{6}$	$\frac{1}{12}$	$\frac{1}{40}$	$\frac{11}{42}$	$7\frac{11}{12}$	$\frac{5}{16}$	$7\frac{10}{21}$	$6\frac{3}{4}$	$13\frac{1}{2}$	$5\frac{5}{8}$	$2\frac{7}{8}$	$1\frac{1}{2}$
$\frac{8}{21}$	$\frac{1}{14}$	$\frac{17}{28}$	$\frac{1}{16}$	$4\frac{5}{6}$	$24\frac{1}{16}$	$1\frac{17}{20}$	$4\frac{11}{18}$	$4\frac{17}{30}$	$25\frac{5}{6}$	$1\frac{1}{6}$	$11\frac{3}{16}$

Answers

Section Diagnostic Test, page 15

$$\frac{7}{9} - \frac{4}{9} = \frac{1}{3} \qquad \frac{11}{15} - \frac{8}{15} = \frac{1}{5} \qquad \frac{3}{4} - \frac{1}{4} = \frac{1}{2} \qquad \frac{9}{14} - \frac{5}{14} = \frac{2}{7} \qquad \frac{8}{9} - \frac{4}{9} = \frac{4}{9}$$

Like Denominators

$$\begin{array}{r} \frac{7}{8} \\ -\frac{5}{8} \\ \hline \frac{1}{4} \end{array} \qquad \begin{array}{r} \frac{15}{16} \\ -\frac{7}{16} \\ \hline \frac{1}{2} \end{array} \qquad \begin{array}{r} \frac{17}{20} \\ -\frac{9}{20} \\ \hline \frac{2}{5} \end{array} \qquad \begin{array}{r} \frac{11}{12} \\ -\frac{3}{12} \\ \hline \frac{2}{3} \end{array} \qquad \begin{array}{r} \frac{5}{11} \\ -\frac{3}{11} \\ \hline \frac{2}{11} \end{array}$$

$$\begin{array}{r} \frac{1}{2} \\ -\frac{1}{4} \\ \hline \frac{1}{4} \end{array} \qquad \begin{array}{r} \frac{5}{6} \\ -\frac{3}{4} \\ \hline \frac{1}{12} \end{array} \qquad \begin{array}{r} \frac{1}{3} \\ -\frac{2}{15} \\ \hline \frac{1}{5} \end{array} \qquad \begin{array}{r} \frac{2}{5} \\ -\frac{1}{4} \\ \hline \frac{3}{20} \end{array} \qquad \begin{array}{r} \frac{11}{14} \\ -\frac{2}{7} \\ \hline \frac{1}{2} \end{array}$$

Unlike Denominators

$$\begin{array}{r} \frac{1}{2} \\ -\frac{3}{7} \\ \hline \frac{1}{14} \end{array} \qquad \begin{array}{r} \frac{7}{9} \\ -\frac{1}{2} \\ \hline \frac{5}{18} \end{array} \qquad \begin{array}{r} \frac{6}{7} \\ -\frac{1}{3} \\ \hline \frac{11}{21} \end{array} \qquad \begin{array}{r} \frac{11}{12} \\ -\frac{5}{6} \\ \hline \frac{1}{12} \end{array} \qquad \begin{array}{r} \frac{2}{3} \\ -\frac{5}{12} \\ \hline \frac{1}{4} \end{array}$$

$$\begin{array}{r} 22 \\ -15\frac{1}{2} \\ \hline 6\frac{1}{2} \end{array} \qquad \begin{array}{r} 11\frac{5}{6} \\ -7\frac{5}{12} \\ \hline 4\frac{5}{12} \end{array} \qquad \begin{array}{r} 23\frac{6}{7} \\ -14\frac{2}{3} \\ \hline 9\frac{4}{21} \end{array} \qquad \begin{array}{r} 9\frac{3}{4} \\ -6\frac{1}{3} \\ \hline 3\frac{5}{12} \end{array}$$

Mixed & Whole Numbers

$$\begin{array}{r} 28\frac{3}{5} \\ -16\frac{9}{10} \\ \hline 11\frac{7}{10} \end{array} \qquad \begin{array}{r} 37\frac{3}{8} \\ -5\frac{3}{4} \\ \hline 31\frac{5}{8} \end{array} \qquad \begin{array}{r} 8\frac{1}{3} \\ -7\frac{1}{2} \\ \hline \frac{5}{6} \end{array} \qquad \begin{array}{r} 18\frac{4}{9} \\ -\frac{2}{3} \\ \hline 17\frac{7}{9} \end{array}$$

PRACTICE SHEET, PAGE 16.

$\frac{1}{6}$	$\frac{1}{8}$	$\frac{1}{2}$	$\frac{1}{15}$
$\frac{8}{15}$	$\frac{12}{35}$	$\frac{1}{12}$	$\frac{2}{9}$
$\frac{3}{14}$	$\frac{3}{5}$	$\frac{3}{5}$	$\frac{1}{10}$
$\frac{15}{64}$	$\frac{1}{4}$	$\frac{7}{12}$	$\frac{5}{7}$
$\frac{2}{3}$	$\frac{1}{20}$	$\frac{3}{10}$	$\frac{2}{9}$
$\frac{1}{7}$	$\frac{8}{35}$	$\frac{21}{100}$	$\frac{3}{16}$

PRACTICE SHEET, PAGE 17.

$\frac{3}{4}$	$\frac{13}{28}$	$\frac{7}{15}$	$\frac{9}{28}$
$\frac{1}{5}$	$\frac{1}{3}$	$\frac{1}{4}$	$\frac{15}{49}$
$\frac{1}{2}$	$1\frac{19}{25}$	$\frac{1}{15}$	$\frac{5}{21}$
$\frac{9}{16}$	$\frac{3}{22}$	$\frac{3}{44}$	$\frac{1}{24}$
$\frac{3}{5}$	$\frac{9}{22}$	$\frac{3}{4}$	$2\frac{1}{4}$
$\frac{3}{64}$	$\frac{2}{5}$	$\frac{4}{7}$	$\frac{8}{9}$

PRACTICE SHEET, PAGE 18.

3	$5\frac{1}{4}$	$\frac{4}{25}$	12
$\frac{2}{3}$	28	22	84
$7\frac{1}{2}$	$13\frac{1}{7}$	$57\frac{1}{2}$	$1\frac{7}{8}$
$5\frac{17}{96}$	$12\frac{1}{2}$	$1\frac{7}{9}$	$2\frac{7}{24}$
$8\frac{8}{15}$	$7\frac{1}{2}$	$1\frac{5}{9}$	$3\frac{9}{16}$
$15\frac{3}{10}$	$10\frac{1}{5}$	$20\frac{5}{12}$	$3\frac{9}{20}$

31

Answers

PRACTICE SHEET, PAGE 19.

$1\frac{1}{6}$	6	33	6
93	22	101	$5\frac{13}{16}$
$1\frac{17}{18}$	10	$45\frac{1}{2}$	$14\frac{3}{8}$
$6\frac{4}{7}$	$20\frac{4}{7}$	$39\frac{3}{5}$	$1\frac{1}{4}$
$11\frac{7}{8}$	$10\frac{1}{8}$	$39\frac{6}{7}$	$5\frac{5}{12}$
$10\frac{5}{8}$	$\frac{16}{45}$	$17\frac{1}{20}$	156

PRACTICE SHEET, PAGE 21.

$\frac{1}{2}$	$1\frac{1}{2}$	2	$\frac{4}{9}$
$1\frac{1}{3}$	$\frac{8}{9}$	1	$\frac{1}{2}$
$1\frac{1}{15}$	$1\frac{1}{2}$	$\frac{4}{5}$	$\frac{3}{4}$
$\frac{16}{21}$	$\frac{1}{3}$	$1\frac{2}{3}$	$\frac{3}{4}$
1	$\frac{9}{10}$	$\frac{1}{3}$	$\frac{1}{7}$
2	$2\frac{11}{12}$	$\frac{1}{2}$	$\frac{1}{4}$

Section Diagnostic Test, page 20.

$$\frac{1}{3} \times \frac{1}{2} = \frac{1}{6} \qquad \frac{3}{8} \times \frac{1}{2} = \frac{3}{16} \qquad \frac{9}{10} \times \frac{3}{5} = \frac{27}{50} \qquad \frac{5}{6} \times \frac{7}{8} = \frac{35}{48}$$

Fractions x Fractions

$$\frac{2}{3} \times \frac{3}{4} = \frac{1}{2} \qquad \frac{15}{16} \times \frac{2}{3} = \frac{5}{8} \qquad \frac{1}{12} \times \frac{4}{5} = \frac{1}{15} \qquad \frac{6}{7} \times \frac{5}{6} = \frac{5}{7}$$

$$\frac{2}{5} \times 50 = 20 \qquad 12 \times \frac{9}{12} = 9 \qquad 4 \times \frac{11}{12} = 3\frac{2}{3} \qquad \frac{2}{15} \times 15 = 2$$

$$5\frac{1}{4} \times \frac{2}{9} = 1\frac{1}{6} \qquad 3\frac{1}{2} \times \frac{4}{9} = 1\frac{5}{9} \qquad \frac{5}{8} \times 3\frac{1}{2} = 2\frac{3}{16} \qquad \frac{3}{4} \times 6\frac{11}{12} = 5\frac{3}{16}$$

Fractions, Mixed Numbers, and Whole Numbers

$$6\frac{3}{8} \times 2\frac{2}{5} = 15\frac{3}{10} \qquad 1\frac{1}{2} \times 2\frac{3}{8} = 3\frac{9}{16} \qquad 4\frac{1}{8} \times 5\frac{1}{3} = 22 \qquad 8\frac{1}{2} \times 1\frac{1}{4} = 10\frac{5}{8}$$

$$6\frac{3}{7} \times 6\frac{1}{5} = 39\frac{6}{7} \qquad 3\frac{1}{10} \times 5\frac{1}{2} = 17\frac{1}{20} \qquad 2\frac{2}{7} \times 2\frac{7}{8} = 6\frac{4}{7} \qquad 12\frac{1}{3} \times 2\frac{3}{5} = 32\frac{1}{15}$$

Answers

$\frac{1}{2}$	$\frac{3}{10}$	$1\frac{1}{2}$	$1\frac{1}{5}$
$\frac{2}{5}$	$3\frac{8}{9}$	$\frac{9}{14}$	$1\frac{13}{32}$
$1\frac{1}{4}$	$1\frac{2}{3}$	$2\frac{1}{2}$	$\frac{32}{75}$
$3\frac{3}{5}$	$1\frac{1}{3}$	$\frac{14}{15}$	$\frac{5}{6}$
$\frac{2}{9}$	$1\frac{4}{5}$	$\frac{5}{6}$	$1\frac{1}{10}$
$\frac{2}{3}$	$1\frac{1}{14}$	$1\frac{3}{10}$	$1\frac{1}{9}$

$\frac{1}{4}$	80	$\frac{3}{10}$	$4\frac{1}{2}$
$\frac{1}{8}$	$\frac{3}{20}$	$2\frac{1}{8}$	$\frac{1}{4}$
$\frac{1}{16}$	$\frac{2}{11}$	2	$13\frac{1}{2}$
8	$5\frac{1}{3}$	$1\frac{3}{10}$	$\frac{2}{3}$
$\frac{7}{9}$	$2\frac{19}{22}$	3	$\frac{1}{6}$
$1\frac{2}{7}$	2	$1\frac{1}{2}$	$\frac{28}{29}$

Section Diagnostic Test, page 25.

$\frac{1}{6} \div \frac{1}{8} = 1\frac{1}{3}$ $\frac{1}{2} \div \frac{1}{3} = 1\frac{1}{2}$ $\frac{1}{10} \div \frac{2}{5} = \frac{1}{4}$ $\frac{1}{3} \div \frac{3}{4} = \frac{4}{9}$ Fractions ÷ Fractions

$8 \div \frac{1}{10} = 80$ $1\frac{7}{10} \div \frac{4}{5} = 2\frac{1}{8}$ $\frac{3}{4} \div 4\frac{1}{8} = \frac{2}{11}$ $1\frac{1}{2} \div 5 = \frac{3}{10}$

Mixed & Whole

Numbers ÷ Fractions

$3\frac{1}{2} \div 14 = \frac{1}{4}$ $1\frac{5}{8} \div 1\frac{1}{4} = 1\frac{3}{10}$ $\frac{1}{2} \div 10 = \frac{1}{20}$ $7\frac{1}{3} \div 11 = \frac{2}{3}$

$10\frac{1}{8} \div 1\frac{1}{2} = 6\frac{3}{4}$ $1\frac{4}{9} \div 2\frac{1}{2} = \frac{26}{45}$ $3\frac{1}{4} \div 2\frac{1}{2} = 1\frac{3}{10}$ $7\frac{2}{5} \div 5\frac{2}{3} = 1\frac{26}{85}$

Mixed Numbers ÷

Mixed Numbers

$6\frac{1}{3} \div 4\frac{5}{12} = 1\frac{23}{53}$ $1\frac{1}{6} \div 2\frac{11}{12} = \frac{2}{5}$ $8\frac{2}{3} \div 6\frac{1}{2} = 1\frac{1}{3}$ $3\frac{1}{10} \div 4\frac{3}{10} = \frac{31}{43}$

Answers

$2\frac{1}{4}$	$1\frac{67}{108}$	$\frac{2}{5}$	$\frac{26}{45}$
$1\frac{3}{10}$	$\frac{77}{150}$	$1\frac{2}{5}$	$3\frac{1}{33}$
$1\frac{15}{29}$	$6\frac{3}{4}$	$1\frac{13}{48}$	$1\frac{1}{9}$
$\frac{11}{21}$	$1\frac{1}{4}$	$\frac{52}{63}$	$\frac{18}{35}$
$1\frac{11}{117}$	$4\frac{13}{35}$	5	$\frac{3}{4}$
$1\frac{23}{53}$	$1\frac{26}{85}$	$1\frac{1}{3}$	$\frac{31}{43}$

$5\frac{3}{4}$	$\frac{3}{5}$	$\frac{3}{14}$	$\frac{4}{9}$	
$1\frac{5}{12}$	$\frac{11}{18}$	$15\frac{1}{21}$	$44\frac{9}{20}$	$15\frac{7}{24}$
$\frac{3}{20}$	$\frac{13}{30}$	$21\frac{11}{16}$	$1\frac{17}{20}$	$11\frac{3}{16}$
$\frac{9}{22}$	$10\frac{1}{8}$	$1\frac{1}{6}$	$7\frac{1}{2}$	
$6\frac{4}{7}$	10	$1\frac{7}{9}$	$57\frac{1}{2}$	
2	$\frac{9}{10}$	$\frac{1}{3}$	$\frac{32}{75}$	
$\frac{1}{4}$	$1\frac{3}{10}$	$1\frac{3}{10}$	$\frac{2}{5}$	

Final Assessment Test, page 27.

The **Final Assessment Test** is arranged horizontally by skills.

Addition

$$1\frac{3}{4} + 1\frac{3}{4} = 3\frac{1}{2}$$

$$\frac{15}{16} + \frac{15}{16} = 1\frac{7}{8}$$

$$\begin{array}{r} 12\frac{1}{3} \\ + 7\frac{7}{15} \\ \hline 19\frac{4}{5} \end{array}$$

$$\begin{array}{r} \frac{2}{3} \\ + \frac{1}{7} \\ \hline \frac{17}{21} \end{array}$$

$$\begin{array}{r} 4\frac{3}{5} \\ + 2\frac{1}{6} \\ \hline 6\frac{23}{30} \end{array}$$

$$\begin{array}{r} 9\frac{3}{5} \\ + 1\frac{1}{8} \\ \hline 10\frac{29}{40} \end{array}$$

Subtraction

$$\frac{15}{16} - \frac{9}{16} = \frac{3}{8}$$

$$\frac{3}{4} - \frac{1}{4} = \frac{1}{2}$$

$$\begin{array}{r} \frac{4}{5} \\ - \frac{1}{2} \\ \hline \frac{3}{10} \end{array}$$

$$\begin{array}{r} \frac{7}{8} \\ - \frac{7}{12} \\ \hline \frac{7}{24} \end{array}$$

$$\begin{array}{r} 23\frac{1}{7} \\ -15\frac{2}{3} \\ \hline 7\frac{10}{21} \end{array}$$

$$\begin{array}{r} 10\frac{3}{8} \\ - 4\frac{3}{4} \\ \hline 5\frac{5}{8} \end{array}$$

Multiplication

$$\frac{2}{3} \times \frac{3}{4} = \frac{1}{2}$$

$$1\frac{1}{3} \times 1\frac{1}{3} = 1\frac{7}{9}$$

$$3\frac{3}{4} \times \frac{1}{2} = 1\frac{7}{8}$$

$$\frac{3}{7} \times 28 = 12$$

$$\frac{4}{5} \times \frac{15}{16} = \frac{3}{4}$$

$$\frac{1}{2} \times 20\frac{1}{4} = 10\frac{1}{8}$$

$$3\frac{3}{5} \times 2\frac{5}{6} = 10\frac{1}{5}$$

$$2\frac{3}{10} \times 1\frac{1}{2} = 3\frac{9}{20}$$

Division

$$\frac{3}{4} \div \frac{1}{2} = 1\frac{1}{2}$$

$$\frac{1}{2} \div \frac{1}{3} = 1\frac{1}{2}$$

$$\frac{11}{12} \div \frac{5}{6} = 1\frac{1}{10}$$

$$\frac{5}{9} \div \frac{1}{7} = 3\frac{8}{9}$$

$$8 \div \frac{1}{10} = 80$$

$$\frac{3}{4} \div 4\frac{1}{8} = \frac{2}{11}$$

$$5\frac{1}{4} \div 2\frac{1}{3} = 2\frac{1}{4}$$

$$1\frac{4}{9} \div 2\frac{1}{2} = \frac{26}{45}$$